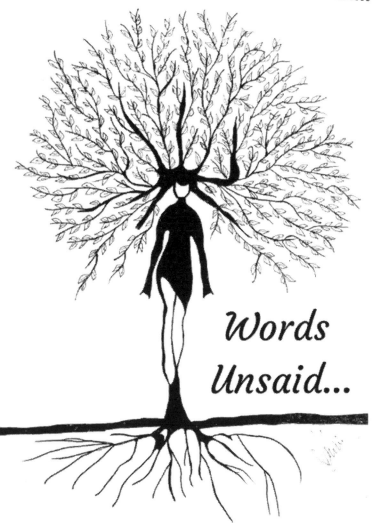

Words Unsaid...

Author: Shivi Goyal

Words Unsaid…

Dedication

To the GODSEND and the eternal mystery of words
that stimulated me to complete the book.

Contents

Words of Appreciation

Media coverage from an eminent newspaper and media agency in India – Dainik Bhaskar (DB Corp).

****

A splendid collection of poems and verses, depicting unknown aspects of pure love. A very odd relation between Love and Weed had us stuck in a multitude of emotions. A must-read.

White Falcon Publishing Solutions LLP

****

"Splendid literary work from the talented Shivi. A bestseller in the making, her words continue to weave magic"

NE8x Inspire (LitFest)

****

Shivi writes with so much thought and one can resonate with her. Life is unexpected we here today we don't know about tomorrow but somethings stay on... and Shivi's work is one much, it's here to stay. Magnanimous, Melting and Mellow all capturing the moment of time. Kudos to you and your good work...

Vaibhav Bhargav
Consultant Chef, Food Stylist

****

I, as a reader, don't favour poetry as it gets somewhat profound, however, 'Love vs Weed' is one such poetry book that has a blend of everything, be it love, desire torment, trouble, highs, lows, outrage rage, depression. Also, how might I disregard the carefully assembled representations which give an appeal to the poems. Best of luck for your upcoming book.

Kitabi_Keedha

Acknowledgement

This book is a brainchild of an exchange of thoughts between two individuals that appeared on a lovely rainy day, savoring a cuppa of espresso. The words floated and there was a hymn of melody. With this, the berry for this publication got started. It's presence itself began with a few unsaid words. Later it got conceived in **WORDS UNSAID.**

I would want to acknowledge my previous publishers–White Falcon Publishing for upholding my initial book launch and publishing it in paperback. I'm still thankful for Amazon and Kindle versions that allow a wide platform to the poets and authors who aspire to broadcast their publication with relatively no money in the pocket. Thankful to my lenders who supported monetarily for printing and also in my vision of being an author and writer.

I'm beholden to all my readers who drove my first book's success. I stand by my critics, which was a learning curve for me. A huge thank you to Starbucks outlets of Mumbai (Lokhandwala and Inorbit Mall and their team) which was my hidden destination for settling and assembling my objectives when I have to gust aside from the hustle and bustle.

I acknowledge my sincere respect and praises to my mom. I'm gratified with my girl's help and encouragement. Although she is just 11 and grouchy but YEAH, she is an excellent individual with support and power. My gratitude to all my clan and family members who have continued their support from my first book got launched and expecting that this time too they would stay by my side.

This would have not been conceivable without my editor, proof-reader, my judge—My companion who has been a steady backbone. He has been exceedingly demanding of my poems/works/stories, and I know how many drafts I struggled on. If I have missed anybody, accept my apologies, but trust me, you all who have been correlated with me on my social media platforms and otherwise are my allies, and I offer my acknowledgment to all of you.

I praise all those communities who stimulated others to be a part of the revolution and strengthen a vent. I'm grateful to those who transformed the lives of others by setting an example for them to live. Thank you all who have empowered or will empower others with gentleness and morality. If you are doing so, then the motive of the book will be a success.

Have you enriched a soul today? Have you entrusted a thought today? Have you empowered a life today?
Start Now!

****

Preface

Welcome, all with heaps of good fortune and love!
Be Happy:)

Studies disclose that literature can intensify emotional intelligence and subdue loneliness, two major perks that can uplift our daily lives. Beginning our day with a chosen poem can have the same powerful impact as other practices, like prayer, meditation, or yoga practice. It entices us to set purposes and free ourselves to the pious world.

Poetry helps us construct our damage, bitterness, and our depression, in the setup of free verse, haiku, iambic pentameter. It obliges us to defy our innermost anxieties and passions, and yields an enjoyable format to be adequate to share them with others. This book will delve into the power of words in the form of poetry, prose, quotes, stories and illustrations in our contemporary society.

Words can excite all of us and ground us; they can give us hope and could serve as our best pals in challenging times. Particularly words are **EVERYTHING** that we mean to claim and aspire to convey. 2020 we saw the widening popularity of poetry throughout the coronavirus pandemic. It forced the writers and poets who had certain strategies for putting up splendid work, took a halt due to pandemic. But their words did not end here. However, this book will also reveal some words which have a profound understanding of distinctive facets of personality.

How many times we all get the strong yearning to convey something. How many times we genuinely yearn to offer our emotions and communicate through different emotional and psychological powers, but could not. This book is a precedent of such opinions, which we all might have experienced in our lives.

This book is all about love, passion, aspirations, friendship, healing, women, despise, mental health, rage, and everything else which periodically is pulled back or unsaid. It is not a scholarly or lyrical type of poetry. The book has prose and poems that would appeal to the modern world and would strike the chord with all those who have felt all the above emotions in their times. You will spot a narrative style of compositions that will offer engagement and intricate explanation about the perceptions experienced.

I will be delighted if you could salvage some pure moments of fortitude and vigour from these words jotted down in the book. Also, I'm confident you would! Will catch you soon with another exciting journey of words and life.

****

Humble Request To All My Readers

Poetry is like an art. It is a powerful medium to express the unsaid. Although there are several other mediums to do so, poetry and expressive words are like an art depicted to raise our concern for certain issues, which we usually cannot say it at the right point in time. I want my readers to have an unbiased view on the collection of poetry written in this book. *I have tried to cater to topics which are un-shared. It contains poems, prose, verses and short stories which will relate to the world's notions of life and love.* The words will make you realize the actual strength which we all have and that is hidden deep down in all of us. Yes, it may have some elements of pain, anger, love, lust, happiness, sadness, depression, and many more, but you will have a solution to come out of it or would help you retain your missing happiness and inner strength.

My request is not to treat the words women biased. These are a pure picture of emotions and incidence happening around all of us. That is not being shared or said.

Another request is not to treat this book as a grammar book. Writing is subjective and is like an art. Literature is a part of any language, as with English. The syntax and syllables are written as per the writers' personification, imagination and experience. Thus, I request you all not to judge the book with grammar or please do not be grammar Nazi. Read it, relate it, feel it, and spread it. The words will do wonder on their own.

Spread empathy. Spread love. The world needs empathy and love. My only intention to come up with this book with literary poetic book, that has short write-ups in the form of stories, and some illustrations to connect closely to all of you. I would be happy if a few handfuls of you would love and read it and would share happiness and empathy to your surroundings.

Last but not the least, whenever you read this book, do not forget to take a picture and put it on Instagram and tag me *@authorontravel* This will help me pay my gratitude to you and I will connect with genuine and like-minded people.

You can also email me at *shivimuskan@gmail.com* or can check my website www.spiritedblogger.com, here you can find my travel blogs and journeys and much more.

My aim is to build a squad of cheerful people and make people smile always.

On this note, I would like to mention about my first book Love vs= Weed, which was released on Amazon and Flipkart worldwide last year. This little book is my first creation in the world of Authors. I feel blessed and thankful to the universe for making this happen*. Love vs= Weed is all about love and its shades. A beautiful collection of poems and prose that depicts the Author's perspective of love and its' shades. It did well, and I appreciate everyone who has read it and spared time to review it. The ones who haven't read it yet, please check the links below.*

My Book: Love vs=Weed available on Amazon and Flipkart

Author page: amazon.com/author/shivigoyal

#authorontravel #lovevsweed #spiritedblogger #shivigoyal

See you soon with tags and emails. Stay connected and close.

The path to awakening and spirituality is your soul.

******

Something Worth Living For

The idea is not

to endure endlessly,

Who prefers to do so,

but the idea is to

form a life,

something worth

living for.

The Moment I Met Him

I used to feel that I could live alone

and I do not need anyone

not even a friend in my life

I used to think I could be alone for all my decisions

I do not need support;

I used to assume I could manage my own finances

I do not need a lending hand

I used to suspect that I could urge my sensuality alone

I do not need a mate

I used to feel satiated while eating supper alone

I used to feel all is well in me when I'm alone

But I was proved mistaken

The moment I met him;

Now, as years passed, he keeps on proving me wrong

And now, I love to be proved wrong again and again

Forever…

****

Making Life Worthy

If you are not living the life you want to live

Then you are stuck in the mess, which you don't even

realize, That you are in...

Beating Self-Respect

To hell with patriarchy
Is what she would say
To watch the men around her
She could not gauge the meaning
But whenever hear it from the elders
She would say to hell with patriarchy.

One day she realised and experienced something which
made her
Literally to howl out intensely and would say, I give a fuck
to patriarchy
And this society…
Questioning herself, as not getting answered from the
patriarchs in the family
This little teen, quested and trenched herself like this…

My heart doesn't want to get imprisoned by
Touching feet of men who do not deserve respect
She would think if he could molest me

And touch me the way I did not want to be

Then to hell with patriarchy.

I allow my body to live the way I want to

And I love the bruises on my body that are due to my

hard work

Which are because of my mensural cycles

But I do not love bruises on my body

Given by men who just want a body

With no emotions, love, compassion and empathy

Then she would say to hell with patriarchy.

Sometimes she would feel that little grass in my garden is

like me

The moment it is grown above the wall

And try to mingle up with other shrubs around

The gardener would come cut it, just because the grass

wanted to grow

Well, I'm like it, the moment I raise my voice against

injustice

Or something which is not relevant as per what the
others wish to,

My words and feelings would get chopped by the men in
the house

So, what about the women in the house?

Are they like that little grass?

Or they are customized to be chopped and thrown away

If yes, then she would disagree

And would say to hell with patriarchy.

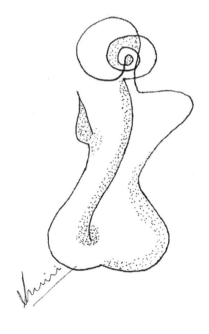

From Man Of The House To Woman Of The House

While growing up in a small town of India with all the love showered on her, she never thought she would become the man of the house. This little chirpy and bubbly girl (Naina) would go to school and would complete her studies with extreme dedication. She used to love going to the farms with her uncle and aunts in the house. She was the one who was the most pampered. When she got her first periods, she was devastated and could not take this fresh change in her body. With all her joyous routine, there was something she would ask her mother daily before sleeping.

When she would not get the desired or satisfactory answer she would sleep with unanswered and manipulative thoughts. Gradually she started getting dreams of the things happening in the house and her surroundings. Her subconscious got accumulated with an array of thoughts and dreams which were not pleasant all the time, started pouring in.

As she kept on growing, her curiosity about things happening around her grew. She still would not get the answer, but one thing was sure that whatever she was developing in her thoughts was evident to the society's norms and customs. While observing all these incidences she could gauge the unpleasant activities which she was not in the agreement for sure.

What were those? What was the thing she was observing? Why was she inquisitive?

They treated the women in the house like secondary elements. The ladies were not supposed to eat until the man of the house eats their dinner. Being in the joint family, the women and especially the "bahus" (the daughters-in-law) were the most vulnerable and were supposed to cook, clean, manage all the household work. So what's the big deal in it, you must think, this is what Indian patriarchy is all about. And this is how we all have been grown up. On top of it, she could not sleep with oozes and unpleasant noises from the bedroom.

This little girl saw the bleeding women sitting in the corner and being treated as untouchables during their mensural cycles. This is not the end yet. We all know that this is reality, and it persists in rural India. It has glimpses in the metropolitan sections, which is quite disturbing. This deep-rooted patriarchy in India has to end.

Who will end it? Girls like Naina, who is just a teen and does not have any power and authority on the system or in the family. But these defined girls are the real rebel and existential threat to these kinds of male chauvinism and misogyny. Because when they would learn and grab the knowledge, they will be fierce and would question not only the family but the entire system of patriarchy.

She did, and she throttled the entire house and later influenced her surroundings as well. A quarter of a century later, when she became a renowned professor and an esteemed life coach, she started teaching and preaching people around to break the chains of patriarchy and relish freedom. She also raised her voice about the minors getting sexually molested and raped. From racism to girl education, she fought for justice starting from the house.

And I must say when the fight initiates from the house and you have to fight with your own family – it is daunting and traumatic. But, years passed, and she never gave up, because she knew if she would give up now, how she would influence other girls sitting in other part of the world. It is a chain reaction. She pulled it over and changed the perspective of many men as well. That brought a lot of change in educating and bringing up girls in urban and rural areas. It still exists, I would say, yes it does.

Thus, several other girls like Naina has to fight for their own safety, security, and self-respect. Hence, destabilizing the issues, and fighting for the concept of "freedom" and equality, she became the man of the house. She took these words in her book later, asking and telling the crowd from being "unfree" to "free" the choice was tough. (Wait for the author's book on the same).

Breaking the norm of "Man of the house" to "Woman of the House" wasn't easy, but the contagious zeal and endless positive energies made everything obsolete.

Being A Woman Is Not A Crime

To Bleed is not a crime

For not to be like a fairy or princess, is not a crime

To have a chubby and outburst body is not a crime

To wrestle for our own good is not a crime

To struggle for their choices is not a crime

To fight for freedom is not a crime

So why only men have the pleasure and privilege of it,

Being a woman is not a crime.

The Magical Night

The Magical Night

The cosmic solace,

Why I love it so much,

Because it leads me to you, my love,

Where there's just you and me in peace.

I Wish I Could Tell You

Loving you is like worshipping

Touching you is to praise God

Talking to you is like to talking to me

Caring for you is tendering flowers

All my life I just want to make you happy

I want you to make satiated for everything you wish for

Making love to you is like river melting in the arms of a

mountain

"I wish I could do all this to you, forever

And you become mine truly forever."

******

Into The Rights And Wrongs

The life of soul is never-ending

The infinite energy that binds us within;

Is what we look for.

It goes deep in the universe where our souls have no end

There is existence of black hole though

We don't realize that we dig deep

Into the rights and wrongs

That engulfs all of us

Nevertheless, living a self-worth life is the soulful life.

What About The Awakening?

The garment of life

Is like a veil

It covers us all with the masks

Decorated, glittery, colored

Patterns, designs, shapes and attributes

They say it is our attire, our personality.

What about the awakening?

What about the devils which hide beneath the garment?

Under which we all are naked as truth

They need this awakening with the veil

With or without the garment the naked soul shall bring

the real you

"That is real you

That is a real soul."

******

The Fragments Of Humane Life

- Pessimist
- Optimist
- Mystic
- Puritan
- Philanthropist
- Idealist
- Realist
- Feminist

And what not…these fragments decide what we are,
Really?

With every fragment, our soul makes its own path to deal with the world outside

Choosing who are you and what you are is the real challenge

Making it simpler for the soul.

Try it out….

****

The Rising

When you are desperate for something to get in your life

Until you don't get it, you grieve.

You may seek the blessings but you may don't get it

though

Knowing or not knowing the cause,

We all grow and have to…

We have to rise and keep going

To seek the blessings,

And to grow with all you have

All this is to achieve our greater self.

To awaken our inner beauty

To rise in love, not to fall

To awaken our mental health

To condition our minds for the good

To rise beating all the evil deeds

Once this is achieved

The grief and sorrow go to coffin

Then It is the rising…

Unsaid Is Killing

Deep within my heart, I feel for you

I sense the unsaid is killing.

The echo of you taking my name prevails around me

The eyes speak the secrets that are deep engraved

But do you know it is hard to get off from you?

The thoughts of you rush my mind all across

Still, I feel alive within you.

I know it needs courage to say the unspoken

Which I could not gather yet

My body feels bonded with your rapture

I feel contentment in your arms

Yet, unspoken to you.

I admit, I'm afraid to leave you

My diaries are full of lovemaking confrontations

Yet, unspoken about you and me

Entangling in her deep thoughts,

She was waiting for a sign to admit the unspoken

She was afraid to let him loose

She was terrified to lose his aura around her

She awaited to feel crazy and joyful with him again

Until she could say the unspoken

Still, deep within my heart, I feel for you

Until the killing of unsaid went cosmic

What I Wish To Tell You Is...
Wish I Could

On a sunny day, she was sitting in a cafeteria, sipping her favorite coffee. She was devastated and was in deep pain. But she was beautifully dressed, with quite a loud eye makeup, so that no one could see her scars and tears floating from her beautiful and big eyes. She looked around with a smiling face to see if everything is all okay with her and with everyone. Silently taking out her notebook from her black handbag and her black pen, she took a deep breath in pain. And when her words wrote, it took her feelings to a storm that had a lot of questions and situational life lessons.

She looked at him with a smile on her face and uttered, it is the time to say goodbye, I shall leave now. But what I wanted to say is that why you even are talking to me. *I wish I could ask you if you know to whom you are talking to and you are here to fool me again?*

I wish I could ask you will you be staying for long or would run away or it is just a matter of time to keep me strong enough to face which I have not seen. I wish I could tell you I'm not used to getting betrayed, I'm not used to being loved either. I have never been treated like a queen or being pampered or walked on a pedestal. I'm also not familiar with an act of someone showing up on my doorstep with roses and orchids.

She took a sigh of relief, looked out of the window next to her seat and wrote - I wish I could tell you I'm not used to getting picked up for dinner dates, shopping, fancy nights or romantic travel. I don't get long loving messages in the night, pre and postdate. I'm not habitual of the feeling of being someone's special. I don't feel like I'm important to anyone where my opinions and thoughts matter to someone or they even count.

I am not used to the way you look at me, with a charm in your eyes, where all my flaws look beautiful and all my curves hid behind your soulful eyes.

I wish I convey this to you, that, I'm strong but I'm like a coconut shell, hard from outside and soft like muslin from inside. This triggers me more, and each time I feel lonely. I wish I could make you understand how I feel and how much I struggle to be me. I know how to describe myself to you so you don't have to struggle to define me and my life. But I wish you could understand and know that I want you to be in my life forever but only if you wish to cross that line which I did already.

I wish I could tell you to go away if you don't love me or take my life seriously. If you don't, then please go away and leave now and never come back as now I will not give you my heart so you can play with it. I wish I could tell you the moments of my childhood that took me to a toll.

I wish I could tell you that when I needed a family; you were not with me and put me to a hell instead, so I could not survive. Later it took me years to love you back or respect all of them the way it was earlier. This is the reason now, I'm not a family person or wish to go to family gatherings where I feel alone. I'm terrified to have one such in my life where I would be bound to attend or host. I'm afraid of me, I wish I could tell you this.

Now, when I look back, I'm alone, although they exist just to exist. At one point having a joint family was something I have always wanted, but now things have changed a long way.

I wish I could tell you how I hated to be alone or lonely and have looked for love at the wrong places. I was naïve or consider me an amateur. This is the reason now I'm comfortable with my loneliness. It has become my old friend, which was once my enemy. I wish I could tell you that it took me longer to reach here and have sacrificed a lot of things. I wish you understand how hard it is for me to give it up for someone temporary in my life. Let it be my friend now.

I wish I could tell you that because of all these reasons I'm now more attached to my associates who supported and helped me to come out of the shit and have accepted me in my true self when I gave up on my life. No matter how hard I try, I cannot explain how and why they love me so much. Why they wish good for me and what is in me which pulls them towards me. I wish I could get the same love from you.

I wish I could tell you I am protected with my pain and ruins. Because when you broke all my walls and endured me with my agony, then left me all alone to deal with trauma and depression. You are not knowing what you did or you may never know what you did but I wish I could tell you it took me years to rebuild the walls from my ruins and now I'm on the verge to build it brick by brick. *I wish you could understand that it is now dead hard for me to break the bricks, as if one falls I will be in ruins again.*

I wish I could tell you about how my time got futile and every time it passed by, made me feel hopeless and worthless. I wish you could understand about those days of my chumps which got wasted, the nights I could not sleep and passed sitting on my slab in my bedroom. I wish that you could know how he disappeared when needed the most. I wish I could tell you how weak I was with him. After that, I pledged never to feel like that again.

Never mind, still I wish I could let you know if you wish to love me, I love you harder day by day. And one day I will find my share of peace in your arms. Then I will find a place in your heart where once I existed and considered the place filled with eternal love and family. Wish you could understand that this place is pure as water and away from all my pain and agony.

If you wish to love me, I will gradually walk away from the comfort of my isolation and start embracing companionship again. If you wish to love me, I swear I will be with you with all my heart. And I will forget the past and about anyone who came before you in my life and you will be the only one.

I wish I could tell you all of this, but for now I sip my coffee instead and would ask you, 'Hey, how are you doing? How was your day?'

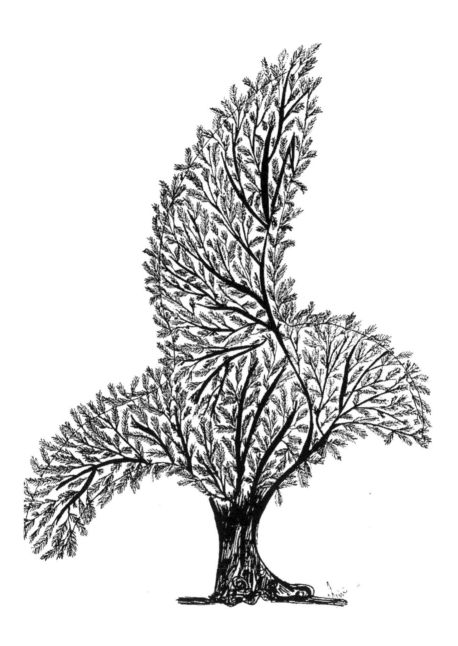

My Darkest Confession

The hide and seek which your eyes play with me

When you are on my body

Is the best game I have ever played?

There can be many reasons to go away

But I would choose the one reason of your sigh

To keep me close to you

Your shadows are like midnight angels

They walk along with me

Never leaving me alone

Your presence is like spirits

My darkest confession

Of How much I miss you

With this hide and seek

I will always find enough light

And love to adore all the pieces of my heart

When I'm with you and you are with me

****

I Would Say – I Live You

In the corner of my heart

You will find me always

That has a special place

Where no one could even gauge in.

When you ask me what you feel for me,

I would say – I live you;

You would ask do you like me,

I would say I love you,

You ask me, do you Wanna be with me?

I would say – I want to breathe you in every second of my life

****

Regrets Of Life

Grieving the moments, she took once upon a time

She craved for them, yet she took,

She was confused; she was a teen,

Later,

Those moments were taken on a ride by pride and hatred.

She kept thinking,

What if I have told you how I felt?

What if I told you that those moments changed my wheel

of life?

Would you still accept me?

Ooh, she was so afraid to fall in love intensely,

For healing, a broken heart will never be easy

She knew this pretty well,

She had been decaying in that hell before,

And now, she doesn't want to be there anymore.

But why is my heart crying in discomfort?

He shuddered...

Why do I feel now that my life is like a hell?

Is there something I did wrong to her?

Should I have to tell her, how much she means to me.

Or

I should have shown her the path of my life

Where she is someone to die for.

Well,

They say some words are better left implicit,

Passions should be retained until they wither.

No, it isn't this way

Because all the cowardice and negativity shall go away

As for saying something of what you feel is the real

bravery.

So what if she won't love me back?

At least there could be moments where I tried.

But it's too late for me to apprehend this truth,

Cause now you're gone and you'll never be mine.

How close you feel when you find someone?

Who is not doomed?

When it grows,

You crave to share so many things

That perhaps you can't usually;

Like,

I recall your eyes glancing at me while I'm dressing up

Your eyes would disclose nothing but love

The facts which you teach me everyday

The things which I took away every night from you,

The touch every night, that would make me fall asleep.

Wish I could tell you I love your care

Every inch of your existence is mine

Wish I could tell you that.

Your face is not dropping me to tell,

How high I feel for your

Time and words will fall short.

But what things you do to me will not

So I'll seek to keep it real.

I want that love we once bestowed

Seldom I want you would express to me

Concerning the elements, you feel

Then maybe sometime I'll understand

How you've acquired to deal?

I've often questioned what it would be like

To feel your warm embrace

To kiss your soft mushy lips

Or have your touch upon my face and neck.

But now I know how amiable is to love you

To touch your skin with me

To feel the purest love

That we share.

I wish I could tell you,

About the time when you kidnapped my heart,

And I got a tinkle to love you.

I wish I could tell you about this,

But, I know deep within, that you

Might break my heart.

Then again, I loved you, liked you

You left without replying a word

It left me behind you

I tried to ignore you

I tried to scorn you

But yet I love you

And it even hurts.

I wish I could tell you to go before you left me,

As I knew you will tear me apart,

But I could not, and I still embrace you

And it still hurts.

I wish I could tell you I certainly loved you.

"What I wish to tell you is… wish I could"

Is Love A Sin?

Is love a sin

Can we say love is a sin?

As whenever she loved someone it was a sin

She covered her face with her hands

But the face got illuminated with a sheer bright light

She could not understand what's happening to her

But still the sky wonders as she was happy

Thinking how in the man's worlds,

Who were holding her tight

She kept on facing the mirror by the thought,

Gushed in her veins off. Is my love a sin?

The shadow spoke...

Do they consider loving humanity being a sin?

Then yes, maybe my love is a sin

If hating cruelty and sexual harassment is a sin

Then yes, maybe my love is a sin.

If putting your words without fear is a sin

Then yes, maybe my love is a sin

If living my self-worth is a sin

Then yes, maybe my love is a sin

If saying NO is a sin,

Then yes my love is a sin.

****

What Do Adam And Eve Tell Us About Love And Sin.

Love is fragile, love is immortal, it is a universal theory of emotions and attraction. But do we all know it's origin? Guess no one knows about it. The thing which we know is about Adam and Eve. Their love story tells us everything about love. The grey and dark shades too. What is the truth of its existence no one could actually claim though? But it is strongly believed that Adam and Eve was the first couple on this planet who brought love as a factor to human civilization. I would like to state a study that has been conducted in Harvard. This survey is famed as Grant Study, in which they surveyed 268 men. They said we took around 75 years, and $20 million spent to come upon a conclusion of five words which explains love in the simpler forms.

"Happiness is Love–Full Stop,"

What does it imply is very clear that anything and everything is love when it yields happiness (of course killing someone is not considered being happiness to the person)? Keep reading to know is love sin or not and what is the true meaning of love since the times of Adam and Eve. Coming from psychology background I have studied the human psychology related to love hormone and oxytocin.

What we know from the times of Adam and Eve is that they were the first to introduce the idea of love in the west and were the first to grapple. The mystery remains of being alive, or the thought of being up-alone. Adam and Eve celebrated this achievement and were happy in their world created by sacred fruits and garden of Eden. They both spread love and humanity and were the essence of single-family.

According to the book of Genesis - The Hebrew Bible, it is believed that initially, they were not given the names, rather they were just created by God's image. Later Adam was asked to eat freely except the–tree of the knowledge of good and evil. When eve was created from one rib of Adam, she was pretty much a part of his life and was a loyal companion of good and humanity. But what happens next is we all know. They both were expelled from the Garden of Eden and considered being the sinners and killers of humanity. The entire history blamed them to bring sin and lust and even death in this world. *This was the greatest and cruellest character assassination in human civilization history ever.*

The ancient myths and creative history take us to the figures of Adam and Eve to grapple with, which was the true existence of a long term and happy relationship in today's world.

What do Adam and Eve teach us about Love?

For sure they did not teach us–Love is a Sin! I have mentioned in the first paragraph about the Harvard study which indicated Happiness is love–full stop. We learn the power of connectivity from Adam and Eve, which is also a psychologically proven emotion in human's life. But the greatest threat to happiness is loneliness, sadness and the feeling of left out. Because when you are happy in today's world, you often are not judged the right way, rather it is indicative to be a jealousy factor as a epxression. Because of the higher percentage of loneliness, we get depression as a by-product. And then, anxiety, hypertension, hostility and worsen heart disease.

This can even lead to death as we tend to be all alone and deprived of love. This also brings social isolation which can lead to severe effects on our mental health, obesity and death.

The first thing God talked about human beings in the Bible, after creating Adam, is ***"It's not right for humans to be alone."*** What we think and modern psychology talks about has been in the Hebrew Scriptures for around 3,000 years back. From Eve's risky reach for knowledge to the unbearable pain of losing a child at the hand of another, the first couple is constantly wrestling with loneliness. By this God wants them to find refuge in each other so they could get solace and forbidden from being thrown out of the garden of Eden.

From where the love and sin came is lively in the scripture of Adam and eve's story. The need for autonomy is an important element of human existence and gives us a phenomenon of equality and freedom in love. Adam and Eve gave us this autonomy. In the field of psychology, autonomy is a pillar of being emotionally healthy and mentally strong. A lot of studies also suggest today that people need a feel of self-directness and want to feel autonomous.

Adam and Eve started being crazy for each other. They were not awkward about their nakedness. ***Eve is "the one," Adam stimulates.*** But Eve yearns for independence, mooches off and eats the fruit. Since the text says she gains acquaintance with this act, but thinkers say that she's seeking more meaning. ***"For Eve, eating the fruit seems to be an autonomous choice."***

The same applies to Adam, who given the option to eat, picks companionship over duty. "He makes the autonomous decision to be with Eve". They learn to oneself–they faced life and death together. They learned to die, to live. It happened only when they fall from grace and faced character assassination, they then fully fall in love with each other (explained by Thomas Merton in his journal).

What psychologists call "Co-narration" — is the last noble quality of romantic love, and the one Adam and Eve are most accountable for preceding. From that second, God divides them in two. They were separated and were liable for writing their own anecdote. This was their first joint byline. Love is a story we tell with another person. It's Co-creation through Co-narration.

Adam and Eve's story is a hint that sometimes the most appropriate wisdom comes from timeless sources. Adam and Eve is the first love story which the civilisation witnessed. *The story we need today, where love and humanity are not SIN.*

Her Mental Strength Was Zero

"The Shadow embraced her in the middle of the night

Her head was heavy, eyes in deep pain, swollen to death

Her mental strength was zero, she shivered

Then, the next moment, she realized she would have her

She left the world in peace and happiness of self-worth"

Value The Inception

The womb is the journey of a girl to a woman, then to a mother. It is the finest feeling which a woman can feel in her entire life. It transforms her from within. Her body transforms from outside and inside. Her organs and her curves drastically change. It fills the entire process with anxiety, nervousness, thrill, stress and curiosity. Although, the journey of pregnancy and then delivery is magical. It is like magic to feel the baby in your hands post the struggle of nine months. This creation is not just a flesh of blood in her body, it is rather full of life and emotions. *"A life within a life"*

The process is daunting for a woman. We say it is different for different women, yes apparently it is true. On the other, whatever shape, size, caste, creed, colour, the age you are, the process of pregnancy is the same for all the women. It is a biological process, but it is emotional, and psychological too. The maternal bond which a mother and child shares during pregnancy are mystical. Some people have quoted that it is more than just a baby growing up, it is something beyond it.

We know that if a woman is pregnant; it is a blessing for her. The birth of a new life in the womb is by choice and considered being a pure life. Another aspect of this journey is not always the same. What I wanted to quote here is the process of inception is not always blissful and pleasurable for all. Couples need a child by choice, they try too hard to get the fetus in the womb. But it does not mean that all the ladies are blessed to have this in the right manner.

Do all the women enjoy this process of inception same as others might do? We all always consider pregnancy as an important part of her life as it is. But do we also pay importance to the journey of making love, foreplay, having sex, and inciting the sperms into her so that the couple can get a healthy and happy baby.

This journey shall be beautiful, like the journey of pregnancy. Some are not blessed with this, though. In our life, we do not talk about it. We feel shy and embarrassed to speak about this part. My personal experience is also not that pleasant in this phenomenon. Whenever I used to speak about sex or the process of inception, the ways, the steps, etc. I was treated as a misfit.

For my whole life, I kept on lingering to this thought and have struggled in family and surroundings to be open about it. But being frank comes with a price. Hence Now I want my child to be an example of unspoken words, which are considered being a taboo in our society. I wish to make her powerful enough to challenge herself and being vocal.

The point is to focus on the origin of life and also to talk and make the origin of a child pleasurable and full of sanity, which many of us are not taking care of. In fact, a lot of them does not even consider thinking about it. Two people mating for a child is like making an artefact from clay. If you do it with full love and purity, the result will be blissful.

Do we consider it? Do we think about it? Do we ever see it as pure lovemaking? Or we just consider it like putting our sperms into her and the job is done!

I'm no one to criticize you all, but to all my readers what I want to focus on is the couples who are not making it happen as a process to be enjoyed, have to forcefully or mindfully think about it. As later this impacts the child's growth and his or her mindfulness. You may believe or criticize me for the same. *(I'm happily accepting criticism).*

Moreover, science has also proven that how the child is conceived ponders impact on how the child raised. It also suggests the parents become towards their children. Now if there are two or three kids and the process differs with the emotion of inception. In this case, all the three then while bringing up will have varied mental stability and parent's perception towards them will also have metamorphoses. For example; you must have seen or heard a lot of stories about differences and fights between kins in one family. Siblings fight and quarrel and parent's interruption is towards one child or they favor one majority of times.

They would favour one more rather than the other. We do not favour the elders much as compared with younger ones. Younger ones are the most loved and pampered, whereas as we see the elder one is supposed to support you in everything without being given credits and appreciation. It can be vice versa too, perhaps, seldom. The stories of these differences can vary.

But the Crux depends on inception, as proven with our biological heirs and genes. So we do not know today that how were we born or the know-how of the process, but was it a result of blissful love, happy marriage, compromised marriage, unmarried, living-in relationship, purely sexual, rape, or marital rape; who would say and who would answer. Lord Shiva only know! When we do not know that how we were born back then. The only thing is science that can help us to understand the genes and biological transformation. Thus, how can we target or question our birth, we can't. In most of the situations, it is the women who are considered being the culprit. Our Indian society put women in the court of motherhood. The contribution is from both the genders though, yet we blame the woman for misfit child or any other unusual thing happening with the child in the house or surroundings. Usually in India it is like – *"Ma ne nahi sikhaya kya" (Your mom did not teach you how to behave and etc.)* Apart from this there are many proverbs and taunts which are prevalent and significantly used in daily lives. These are totally for women, pointing their upbringing and birth. My question is simple, why? And I have been questioning many on this, in my lifetime, but it is deep rooted in our system.

Why?

Gradually, when we grow, we develop to rely on our birth cycle. Unknowingly, of course, as we are ignorant about it. Hatred, criticism, cynical, fear, anger, selfishness, dishonesty, infidelity, revenge–and many more. Feelings and expressions like these inculcate and it becomes tough for us to cope. The irony is for parents to feel helpless in definite situations.

Other than this we see a lot of Psychological and emotional patterns developing in the children which do not seem to be acquired from the external world. Psychiatrists have mentioned that behaviours like arguing, unreasonable questioning, frequent quarrels, degrading others, highly critical, abusive behaviour, manipulating things; result from our birth cycle.

Is there a solution to what has happened in the past? Yes.

All we need to know is our actual worth. The idea is to break the monopoly of the thoughts and bring a change in our thought patterns. We do not want our children to get grown up in a duplicative world. Whatever as parents of that child we have done or faced, we know in fact at the time it is our past life. That makes it a vicious circle of life and its motives. *Eventually Karma rules the world, from present to afterlife.*

There's no one ever could validate our real origin, except medical science. The womb of a mother is the world where you create your life before you come to this world. For all what happens in our lives, we have reasons, but a few questions are only with power. The only thing we can change is our thought process and the way we see things. Admiring mothers, respecting women is the first thing to start the cleansing process.

Valuing womb is like respecting GOD because the journey of GOD has started from a seed and it has passed to human life via woman as a medium. Shiva is not complete without Shakti. It is amalgamation of Shiva and Shakti that created the world. In order to have fulfilled life start respecting the originator. It will lead you to a healthy and happy life, honor mothers, respect womb—*as it is the origin of our life in this universe.*

The Womb

The womb is the only abode where my world is solo

It is a brute reality, which is…. In its own way beautiful.

I find myself seldom in my womb where my baby remains safe

It is actually the fact that we won't understand the life within us until it grows inside you.

The mother then feels that my baby's heartbeat is safe in my womb

Coming out to this world, which is of no one's will make my child weak

My child would think that the life which you have given me is so tiny and fragile, Mom.

Which is subject to the danger of death

But Oh God, hear to the prayer of my mom

To create a life safe and sound.

Later, she prays to you for my safety throughout nine months

God, if you exist, then hear our prayers! Amen!

Our kids should be safe!

Respect Is The Word

Wombs are the dwellings where all of us belong to

It's where we all come from, yeah, we come from

so what we shall do?

we need to be wise and nice,

What we need to do and it would be wise to do that,

Shall respect our women and their wombs in real sense.

Respect Them, yes respect is the word

Which is taken a toll in recent times and too many times,

Although It's taken upon men already

So what we shall do? neglect them,

Degrade them, and even Rape them,

Wow, this is thought-provoking isn't?

Do whatever you want to,

Like women are not the ones who have given birth to

them.

Where'd they come from, if women aren't there?

But do they know or even if they know, do they
understand?

OOH, come on, "understand" itself is a huge word to
these men
Who doesn't know the meaning itself of this word in
depth?

And what women do?
As if they really don't take it upon ourselves
To bear them in their womb for nine months,
She nurtures them, and love them, Yes all of us,
The Wo-men, yet it's very well known to the world
That it takes a powerful woman to raise a vigorous man,
Yes, and the one's who's not going to a little one always
Or be a little vindictive, of what a woman can't or can

*Now the questions are, rather she shall be a frank
person or a dumb ass*
Or she shall be a blunt about the correspondences,
Which the world needs right now,

Ooh, no, it is what we all need at this point in time.

Instead of using rude dismiss-es, yeah, why not?
Mockery for us, and for many of us?

To reflect, to praise, to debate, to protest, for the same
Love and admiration, that a Queen actually shall have
and a king and they believed to live happily ever after…

They would have, right? Believed this way, perhaps,
And there shall be respect, where is the respect?

Where is the mutual respect?
It is simple until we genuinely feel our birth to be divine
and pure
We will not be able to bloom the wombs
As far as the womb blooms our women will be
respected.

Life's Story, Untold To Many

Life is a story

Untold to many

We do not even know

Which is the path

And where it will lead.

Keep following the

Ray of light coming

Straight from the universe

It might help you

To complete your story

In the maddening world.

Super Mom

Mom, you're a terrific mother,
So gentle, yet so powerful.
The many ways you prove you care
Constantly make me feel I exist.

You are patient when I'm irrational;
You give teaching when I call for;
It seems you can do most things;
You're the master of every task.

You're a sturdy source of warmth;
You're my cushion when I stumble.
You help in times of strain;
You uphold me whenever I cry.

I love you more than you know;
You have my unlimited reverence.
If I had my choice of moms,
You'd be the one I'd elect!

Blessing: *I want to thank God and all the energies for blessing me with the best mom in the universe. I wish the same for others. Being a mother feels awesome and complete. I extend my love and blessings to all the moms and their children.*

****

Hope Is A Delusion

It can be the end of the world;

He said no,

She said it can be,

He said I will be there for you, even if it is the end of the world.

She said you will never know;

When the day will come and you will not be able to do anything,

He said—I'm still hopeful and will be there.

She thought—maybe;

She knew down the line that he is right,

But can't help her emotions to flow like a river

Where she is thinking he can be with her but he left;

She felt that hope is just a delusion.

The best thing about Hope is the delusion

The hunches, the assumptions, the predictions, the unforeseen;

Which we think to be foreseen.

The best thing about Hope is the delusion

Just Follow Your Heart

We have heard it many times
I used it many times
Saying it again
With another twist to it
Just follow your heart;

Just follow your heart is all what we should do.
Life gives us chances to follow your heart truly;
It does put us in certain circumstances,
Where the clash of mind and heart exits;
But, the subconscious solution to it
Is to follow our heart, to get to the path.

And when exactly we do not know
Where it is pointing to, it does not tell us even
The only cure then is to,
Just follow your heart
Have you ever thought
Why?

Because our heart is the center of

All the Cosmic energies.

If you believe in them

And keep faith alive

The core remains strong and nurtured.

****

You Gotta Get Your Way

Life is a pond of grief,
Life is very fragile,
We feel loaned up in our lives;
We feel hopeless many times.

Then we wake up every morning,
With a thought that this morning will be beautiful,
And would rock while following our heart;
Will not get upset with external factors,
Think of the smile which makes you smile.

Think of a monk who is spreading love,
Think of the sunshine;
Which is unconditionally spreading light to the world,
And follow your heart.

Think of all the small things,
That give you happiness,

Think for short term goals,

To accomplish today;

Think of becoming a reason for someone's smile,

Think of forgiveness,

You gotta get your way!

There's nothing called as grief

It is all in your mind.

Bonded In The Emotional Euphoria

Deeply in love with him

Yes, passionately in love with him

You make me feel elegant and sexy at the same time

But I miss the dates and await the tide

When you would show me the real you for me

Show me that you love me

Show me how intensely you admire me

Show me how you make me strong

When you feel shattered within

When you are in suffering and pain

The heartbreaks with you are similar

For me, it is likewise

But how do you gather strength to restore it flat?

And give me a shoulder to lean on

Show me the happiness which I could not find

In me, and fail to believe you, in my dreams

Show me how could you be nasty sometimes

When I don't want you to be

Yes, I feel comfortable with you

Bonded in the emotional euphoria!

Show me how you fantasize my touch

You lust for my body and my skin

While you are engulfed in chores deadly

While you are bewildered with the external shit

Just tell me;

Just tell me;

Show me how do you love me so much

As my every hunger gets satisfied

My deep passions are rewarded

And when I open my arms, I find you within in a closet.

You are my refuge and I'm yours

****

Do Not Beg For Love

She was tired;

She was failing;

She thought, she can't keep going

Because she is a woman.

A woman of distress

A woman who is a housewife

A woman who is a mother

A woman who is in disguise

A woman who is born to be disgraced

For her body, for her skin color, for her bulges

For her work, for her voice, for her being vocal about herself

For her being a daughter who can't study much

For her being a girl who does not have the right to be in pinky thoughts

For her being a teen whose assets are precious to her

But not for others who disgrace her

By all the kinds and deeds this society has made her;

Felt like a curse to be a woman

As if she was born beautiful and intelligent

But then she was urged for her afflictions.

For her relationships with her own family

Friends, far-seated relatives, colleagues

And friends of benefits.

For all the occasions where she can't be the host

Was made a host for the society,

For reasons, which she is not prepared for.

For the grace forced on her

For all those moments which shall not be cherished

For all those moments that killed her innocence in her

school bag

For all those moments when she was numb about her

molestation

When she swanked into proximity and was being judged

For sleeping with more than one man

Is it? sounds self-critical

Owing everything to the dear woman

I would say, f**k the world with strength.

Do not beg for love;

Do not beg for respect;

Love comes as a gift.

The ones who don't deserve you to

accept the way you are

F**k them, hard.

You are more precious to yourself

than anyone else in the world.

Tell them loud and clear;

Leave me alone;

Let me bear all the weight on my breasts,

And subtly fume to the life which I will design.

Leave me undone for god's sake just once,

Leave me unprocessed, just don't think about me,

Then I shall remember you once for a reason of love.

For the conversation with two beautiful minds,

Until we meet again.

Provoking Change In The Society

At times, things change

At times, they for good

At times, they change bad

As we think…

Change is the rule of the universe

But then this change does not come with a warning

And things changes.

He said; I thought, I'm not made for love.

She said; I thought he is not made for me either.

They both thought they were not made for this world

And the changes kept on happening without warning

Cloud said; I'm heavy and lofty. Need to burst.

Rains said; Nah, not now the world is not prepared.

Clouds Said; No choice, the burden shall pass away.

And we see thunder, lighting, floods, heavy winds

The dévastation continues, changes continue…

A few strokes here and there

The Tides of creed and caste

Burn the communities;

Provoking change in society,

Preaching wisdom with feather-like tongue.

But do they know?

Their delusion and lack of wisdom

Is destroying the communities,

Based on sex, caste, creed, colour,

But this world has the energies

That govern the universe.

And humans full of wisdom also can't beat it

Thus, one change occurs;

One change dissolves the world into humanity;

It is for us to realise.

Then I Rested My Case

I kept on failing

Failing and failing again

Tumbled and failed again

This kept ongoing

Then I rested my case

Saying I Love You Is Not An Apology

Saying I love you

Is not an apology for what all?

Is being said and done

For years or for those moments;

When I felt helpless,

When I felt hopeless,

And not earnest of my love for you.

I felt extremely distorted;

For not being there with you,

During the times much needed.

For me love is not just a word;

It is like overcoming the obstacles,

Between us or around us.

I foolishly rested my case to the powers;

I wish I could unravel,

Rekindle the moments,

And could make you express,

My everyday love for you.

For the truth is;

Saying I love you,

Is not an apology for what all?

Is being said and done.

I Gave Up Thinking

I used to think too much

That I'm not a good person

That I'm not a good wife

That I'm not a splendid mother

Not a successful daughter

Not a great friend

Not a fantastic employee/employer

Not a person to be with

Then…

I gave up thinking

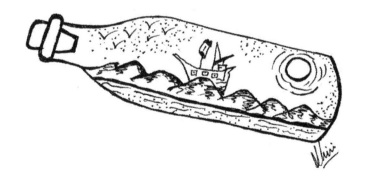

Do Not Doubt The Creator

The universe took its own time on you

To nurture you, to create you.

It then crafted you to give you the;

World you needed,

And desired for,

Think, next when you doubt your own being

Think, next when you doubt the creation of the power.

Because, when you doubt the creation,

You doubt the existence of the power and energy.

Which is superior to everyone else in the world!

When I Kissed You

How would you feel If I say I love you?

In the summer, underneath a maple tree

How would you feel If I say I love you?

Stargazing in the night, when the sunrise would replace

the moon

How would you feel If I say I love you?

Under the silken sheet of muslin, you and me

How would you feel If I say I love you?

Every inch of mine touching yours

How would you feel If I say I love you?

Putting this night behind us forever

How would you feel If I say I love you?

Then he replied,

You may not be my first love

You may not be my first lady

But when I loved you

When I kissed you;

You made all the other loves inappropriate.

The Ocean Of Guilt And Agony

Love is full of dark emotions

Love is full of grey emotions

also not just happy go moments,

The opposite of love is indifference;

For this, you have opened up your heart and mind to

these feelings.

These dark emotions will almost kill you

They will tear you apart, they will give you all the pain

Filled with an ocean of guilt and agony

This feeling of hopelessness and despair

will take to the world of unknown

And this is when you realize,

maybe it is the end of your life

This is where you will gonna end yourself.

So, if love gives you hope, love gives you a reason to live

Love also gives you reason for not living

For struggling in misery and guilt

It also gives you another meaning of hatred

But there is a way out of it

Dunno what the relationship counsellors say;

But if you are battling in a relationship,

And want to get through it. Please follow your heart.

As listening to your mind will not help,

In the sky of melancholy,

hugging helps, caressing each other,

With all the fondness you have for each other will help,

This will give you the virtue to listen

to each other and communicate.

Our heart is a bunch of muscle;

And when it rips, break, it shall get amended as well

In order to set it right in place,

Feel the pain more than you feel the heartbreak,

Deep intense;

The more you bear, sooner it

will be enormous to engulf the world around

That is, full of voluminous emotions.

Love takes everything;

It is just your greatness depends on it

And trust me, when you have the

competence to take charge

Of everything coming your way

Then love takes it overall…

****

It Was Not The Death

For which I was excited for

It was the rotten soul

It was not the bells

I heard in the church

That reminded me of my burial

To meet the almighty

It was not the feeling

That I could not breathe

Throughout midnight

While watching my clock ticking

Majority of the mess

And the chaos in my life

Was limitless and uninvited.

The Rotten Soul

I did not have a key to rekindle

The key to make things right

I did not get a chance to clarify

That my life is not a rotten tomato

To be eaten by none and enjoyed by all

Just a few words…

It was not all about death,

For which I was excited for

It was the rotten soul

To justify my despair to myself and only me

He is Naïve, He Is My Man!

He is Naïve; he is soft

He knows what he does

He is the man who has never loved a woman

The way he does it to me

His heart is of Gold

His touch is like diamonds

I got mad over every single sigh of his touch

He is my man!

Love Is A Stranger

They say love is immortal

It has no language

The sound of every love relationship is faith

Yet why it feels like a stranger to me

Love is that breeze that kisses your pain away

Still, why I feel love is a stranger to me

Love is a treasure

That has a veil of untold moments to cherish

Why do I feel–love is still a stranger thing to me?

It is spiritual

It is mystical

It never lies to you

But it can't be mine forever

She had this feeling always

Knowing that what love is, maybe

But she still kept on thinking

Why?

Love is still a stranger to me!

He Is A Mark On Her Heart

In his eyes, she could see the pain

She could count the scars

She could scan across his heart

Penetrate deep through his heartbeat

She could see where she infuses in him.

Yes, he is a mark on her heart

She stands like a savior back as a voguer

She would stalk for good and would not respond

She would keep all his secrets like a cache

Yes, he is the mark on her heart.

Back then

She would think and sit along the cliff of a mountain

Has she executed a sin

Standing beside him is a sin

To allow him to her love is a sin

Or what mistake has she made by committing "I'm Der"

Why would she think this way?

Because of her overflowing sins and repercussions of the mistakes

She would have made;

Is not granting her to believe that someone can come to make her like

A garden full of flowers,

Where indeed the thorns are turned into rosy mosaic

Yes, he is undoubtedly a mark on her heart

What Is Right And Wrong?

The breeze of love

The subtle whisper of the breeze

Is like the soft touch of almighty

It is like the universe is lurking us to perform love

The breeze pretty behave like a hunter

Making you fool as if nothing has happened

It conveys–please do not pretend to be homeless

Because you are not

Because even I'm homeless

Just savor life, without worrying

What is right and wrong?

The breeze behaves like a kid

Whose innocence is divine

When it blows over your face

And falls perfectly on your face

The best part is, when she looks ravishing

She would smile like a kid

That's the fascination of breeze in life

At times the unsaid becomes evident

As the breeze puts you in a tussle

To listen to your heart or mind

That's the pure magic of nature and love

It is when the universe sees you closely.

You Took All Of Me

I just gave you my friendship

How did you take?

All of me...

For a new journey to begin…

How much wild you want to see her

Depends how much you respect her

life is not perfect for all,
you are the artist to make
it perfect....

Virtual Love

Can we kidnap our love? Can we just be real for some time?

Often it feels like love is just through the screens, tablets, video conferencing and social media. Through satellites, we fall in love. These radars send our wishes and carry our expressions to fill the aching void in all of us. The millennials love it and it is a continuous practice for them. It had kept ongoing and it will keep going and then there will be a silence. We spoke about everything. We were together through our satellite system. We laughed, we chased our dreams. As a girl, I felt as if my body is some celestial body with mass and matter and his too. Waking up virtually, going to bed virtually. *Everything was the same for years. And then we experienced stillness.*

As the summer approached autumn and then the winters made its way with freezing temperatures, our times went to a standstill. I gave my heart to him with a photograph, but sunlight faded it. Our thoughts and dating became blurred, and I became so afraid of losing something which I wasn't sure that was mine or wasn't mine.

And then, with the orbits of the celestial bodies, the rotation of our love changed. The dull and sad whisper was murmured by the chants of birds and shine of the twinkling stars.

I would question myself, that is this a, kick start of my static life with him. By now, we both pulled it over to the moon and our relationship orbit took off virtually again in happiness. I told you it is an ongoing process.

I would still wonder how the other celestial bodies maintained this outpost love. Are there people like me who have been into these state of affairs or have been going through the mayhem of virtual love. Ultimately, the concoction of original love gets hit by moon, and we both knew that it is the one which we can see from the earth in real, not virtual. ***The Moon!***

Love, Benefits And Convenience

She wanted to say and realize that love is the most

beautiful thing that can happen to anyone on this earth...

But Oh My darling;

Love hurts the most

And in today's world,

It is manipulative with our benefits and convenience

Love hurts the most...

The Hard Things To Admit

Admittance is the key to life
Self-worth is the reason to love yourself
Self-respect is respecting oneself
But I have to admit today,

That most of the years
When my life was crumbly
And have faced drastic circumstances,

I actually allowed others to treat me this way
I allowed others to take me for granted;
Eventually, I allowed others to treat me the way I treated myself.

******

Wildflower

She often found herself in a **wild forest**

Surrounded by **thorns and affliction**

She weathered all the storms

She passed all the **oceans of sadness**

She **grew up free** and unpretentious

Seemingly **feeble** and impulsive

But **secretly resilient** and sturdy

Who could withstand all the…

Extreme temperatures of life

The Looted Soul

The last lane

In the end, everything will be fine

The looted soul will merge with its leftover pieces

The embodied love will meet his love at the end of the
lane

The most relevant regret will pass away

The memory lane will remember the unseen

Let the world know the transference story of you and me

Where we would meet in the last lane

****

I'm Not A Feminist

I'm not a feminist. I'm not the one who would always punish or slam men. As an avid reader and writer when I first read *Elizabeth Barrett Browning's–Aurora Leigh a "novel in Verse"* published in 1856, I thought feminism is something about women and to love the core of being in this gender. *This Aurora Leigh by Browning suggests the force of being a woman and how they can transform the world with their right attitude.* I have always been a supporter of women and have always raised a voice for injustice towards inequality and sexual harassment towards women. We face a lot still not given much, we gather all our strength to raise children and the house, and what do we get in return. Just to quote what Aurora's cousin, Romney Leigh, summarizes his attitude toward Browning and women writers of that era: (Refer: Source on last page)

Therefore, this same world
Uncomprehended by you must remain

Uninfluenced by you. Women, as you are,
Mere women, personal and passionate,
You give us doting mothers and chaste wives.
Sublime, Madonnas and enduring saints!
We get no Christ from you, — and verily
We shall not get a poet in my mind.
"Elizabeth Barrett Browning,"

Since the 1960s and before women in all parts of the world have fought for their rights and equal status in society. This revolution is more than 100 years old. In India, too, feminism and fighting for women's justice started in the 19th century. The women fought for civil rights, legal justice, marriages, sexual harassment, equal rights at work etc. it was a political and cultural watershed. During these times we saw a surge of women writers and poets emerging in all parts of the world. *These poets changed the era of writers and women rights.*

The structures and support they have created with their words have profoundly brought a revolution in the world for the women of all castes and creed. Often we consider feminism to be biased as it is about women on the whole. We see a lot of women hate men. In reality, true feminism is just fighting for equal rights. Women need to be equal to men in building the new future. *From #metoo to #BeBoldForChange everything signifies quality in every sector of life for women.*

I know many of you would not agree, but my personal experience has made me learn a lot about women and men. Well, not exactly like men are from mars and women are from Venus. Nothing Like this exists. (Refer: Source on last page) If you guys have read this book; you would know what I'm implying to. That book is also one of an example of quality in total, if interpreted correctly. *If you have not read, I would recommend you all to read it.*

This section of the book will focus on some poems and prose about women and their feminism. It is not a biased approach, yet has a strong inclination of women empowerment and their status in our society. Men won't lose their rights if they would give equal status to women, they why to suppress women.

While writing about body and woman curves my favourite and inspiration is Walt Whitman. His nine-part poem – I sing the body electric glorifies and celebrates the body and its curvatures, structures, stretches, fats, and swollen parts. Another love of mine is Maya Angelou, (Refer: Source on last page) her deep and unapologetic poetry slams the societal norms and brings a warrior in a woman. A few from my collection:

****

Celebrating Woman

Celebrating woman is, celebrating democracy;

Celebrating the body of the woman is celebrating her freedom,

Celebrating the procession of her success is celebrating her reign,

And the delight is her body's mysteries;

That awe everyone

From the lords to the humans

And to the universe

****

Shrinking Within The Walls

Pressed in the corner

Shrinking with the walls

With slightest paper in the hand

Kept assuming

Do they have to be in the present tense every time?

Is this the extant for me?

Is this I'm here for?

Longer days and shorter nights was her thing;

Nevertheless, there was more time for heartbreaks.

If she writes it down

Would anyone read?

If she asks voraciously like a lioness

That…

Is there a rule book for the world's best girl child?

How she has to **behave**

How she has to **dress**

How she has **study**

What she has to **study**

How she should **smile,** even

To whom she shall get married

And so on....

Or whether she is allowed to eat together with family

When in periods?

Is she allowed to fall in love?

Whether she is allowed to chase her dreams

Or even talk about it.

Shrinking into the walls, she questioned

Is there a written rule book which we all are following?

That tells what is right and wrong

That everyone has but not me

 Slowly when the sunshine showered/withered

This flower which was deprived of sun

Got the light of a fire

This flower who was longing to belong to

Strewed all the nectar to someone and everyone

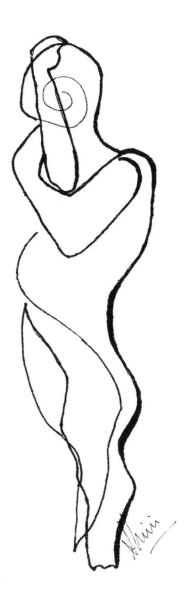

Curves Have No Age

There is no age for a woman to be loved

There is no age bar for a woman to dress-up in a certain way

Well, what's this matter is all about…

We are discussing women

Her **straight lines** are wonderful

Her **curvy buttocks** are luring

Her **brown and dark genitals** are the universe

Her **arms** take all the pain within

Her **breasts** are life saviour

Her **womb** carries the infinite energies

Her **hair when entangled** with anger are unstoppable

When detangled with respect they are yours

What about her **lips and face?**

The **span of her lips** and the slight curl

With **dimples** in the cheeks

Makes her worthy of all the

sexual desires she wishes for

So, whenever you walk into a room

Finding a naked body of a woman

Trust the instincts of love and bliss

Feel the reverence of her assets and charm her

With everything you have to shower on her

Grow Up, Babe

Don't worry you are strong

You are a warrior

Your body is not a crime scene

Your body is not an apology

Your body is like a cliff

It is not easy for everyone

To climb and get over

It takes guts to love a woman

Your spaces between the legs are almighty

Blessing your presence in this world

Your femininity is like a Goddess

Your tresses are like waterfalls

Your every inch is crafted with excellence

Your existence has determined

Our Ancestors' history

The swing of your hips

Is the luck redesigned

Your smile is the soul of the universe

OOH woman…

You are defined and inherited

Indigenously by the powers unarticulated

You are just so wonderful, woman

You are one of them

You are them

Like them

Equal to the men

Because for the creators

There's no inequality

There's no man vs woman

Its center is just life

So, live it up, woman

Grow up, babe

The world will be on your knees

****

Hey Hang On, The Power Said!

Hello ladies,

How are you doing today?

I've heard that the storms are wild

The thundering is wicked

The dazzle seems to be imperfect

What happened?

Ladies answered...

Our daily wages are getting heavy on our work

Our bodies are not deemed

Our pain scream out loud

Our bleeding becomes desperate

Our sexual desires are tainted

Hey hang on, the power said

You are the future

You're the universe of birth

You are the ones who would bring revolution

If you would equip your talent

This will be the legacy for the generations to come

Hello, ladies

Let the ash sublime

Let the quest being

Let the lioness in you rise to

Love, heal, revolt, empower

The ones who left me

The ones who treat me like a honey bee

Took all the honey

Licked, sucked, ate

Leaving the scum behind

We're not the brave ones

We're not the ones with courage

They are the ones

Who made us brave

They gave us strength

To confront the real, them

Today she is daring enough

To conquer

To love her sexuality

To love herself, totally!

There's A Bird Caged In Vanity

All of which is implicit and to be said

Words which I will leave when gone

Letters which I would leave for you

Secret treasures hid in my diaries

There is always something to confide

There's always something to hide

There is something to change

There's something unacknowledged

I wish the world shall know

There's a confession in the words

But when I'm gone, will they matter?

There's story of racism in my closet

There's a bird caged in vanity

There are songs in my diary which are not composed yet

There are carols which haven't recited yet

There are desires unexpressed

Travel journals with the quest unattested

Are on my walls

But will they be said when I'm gone?

I leave the world with all my possessions left

The only thing

Which will be mine

Are my words?

And the only thing which I possess are my words unsaid

Hoping they will be whispered once I'm gone.

Mental Health

Psychologically understanding mental health with some statistics. Mental health refers to cognitive, behavioral, and emotional well-being. It is all about how people think, feel, and behave. People sometimes use the term "mental health" to mean the absence of a mental disorder. Mental health can affect daily living, relationships, and physical health. (Refer: Source on last page), *According to the World Health Organization (WHO):*

"Mental health is a state of well-being in which an individual realizes his or her own abilities, can cope with the normal stresses of life, can work productively, and can contribute to his or her community."

The WHO stress that mental health is "more than just the absence of mental disorders or disabilities." Peak mental health is about not only avoiding active conditions but also looking after ongoing wellness and happiness.

They also emphasize that, preserving and restoring mental health is crucial individually, and throughout different communities and societies the world over.

In the United States, the National Alliance on Mental Illness estimate that almost 1 in 5 adults experience mental health problems each year.

In 2017, about 11.2 million adults in the U.S., or about 4.5% of adults, had a severe psychological condition, according to the National Institute of Mental Health (NIMH). (Refer: Source on last page)

Mental Health In India:

In India, WHO estimates that the burden of mental health problems is 2,443 DALYs (Disability Adjusted Life Years) per 100,000 of the population, and the age-adjusted suicide rate per 100,000 populations is 21.1.

They estimated that, in India, the economic loss, because of mental health conditions, between 2012-2030, is 1.03 trillion dollars.

Mental health workforce in India (per 100,000 population) includes psychiatrists (0.3), nurses (0.12), psychologists (0.07) and social workers (0.07).

Source: WHO (Refer: Source on last page)

Your mental health matters–It's time to change

Do you feel depressed?

Do you get suicidal thoughts?

Do you feel lonely?

Any thoughts like these or related to these emotions are not good for your mental and physical health. The tendency of self-harm could be potentially triggering. The dark shadows and loneliness capture every single thought of yours, leading you to think like hell. The distraction towards all negative around you kills your present and future.

This sinks into your soul and stops it to react in the right direction. The thing with depression is, it will hit you, when you least expect it. Sneaking your mind, winding your thoughts through your body, it will tear you apart. When it occurs, it does not literally show symptoms like fever, but one thing is for sure, the emotional state of self-harm, I'm not good, I'm not a pleasant human, in fact I'm the worst in everything, prevails. Eventually, you feel you have a dirty soul and no one is yours.

And Then……read below!

My Weakness Cannot Be My Undoing

There is a dire need of understanding mental health. Mental health is not sadness; it is a serious disease which itself *says–dis-ease.* Which actually means it can be cured, and the one having mental health issues shall not be disappointed. There is always a reason for your sadness, but all sadness is not mental health. *Thus, understating it, is imperative.*

I was very young, probably in my teens, when I started having responsibility issues. You know, sometimes being responsible gives you a feeling of melancholy. Danish (name changed) clearly recalls his times when in the house and among his family friends he was considered as the most responsible teen. But gradually because of which he started developing a different attitude towards his own people.

The attitude of being the best, at times he would feel burdened with a lot of jobs to do, over-confident, arrogance, etc. All these started reflecting his mental condition, which was evident among his people. This pattern shifted toward his youth, and his workplace got affected terribly. Overburdened with responsibilities made him develop anxiety issues. His perfection led to imperfection and impatience.

He recalls weeping in the washroom. He states today his times of being getting jealous with his colleagues, which impacted his productivity. He started worrying more and became an egotistical person. He would hide in his cubicle and overthink about the job and his work and his appraisal. The pattern which started on a pleasant note in his childhood of making a child responsible for something and a proper warrior in life resulted in drastic mental health problems and behavior issues with Danish.

With life moving ahead, it affected his married and professionally life. The placements and shifting made him more vulnerable as he had to deal with a new set of people. But until then he was gone in the deep bin of mental health problems. At last, when noticed severe changes, he underwent CBT–Cognitive-behavioral therapy. During the times of his diagnosis, he used to feel sad and happy at the same time.

When asked he would say I do not know why this is happening, it had never happened with me. People would ask me, are you upset? What happened? I would say nothing because of my fear of being judged. Thankfully, his friends and family were supportive, else the journey to happiness would have been really tough.

Now he remembers the feeling of sadness and being ignorant about all those emotions that have affected him. He wished that no one would have ever felt this way and if it happens to you, go get it checked. It is ok to be mentally sick or stressed out. Until you won't understand, you won't be able to change the way you think. Until you won't face, you won't be able to let others know about it.

Knowing Mental health is prudent.
Understanding it, is like to treat it
No shame, no hiding, no judgement
Speak about mental health
Raise your voice
Make your weakness your strength

Please Note: *In case you are facing any trouble or have anxiety issues. If you feel alone. If you feel mentally sick and depressed or any other mental issue which you are not able to share with anyone, you can try giving it a shot with me.*

What I want to say here, is if you feel to talk to someone without being judged or misunderstood then you can email me your concern. I have mentioned my email in the beginning—sharing it again (shivimuskan@gmail.com or Instagram @authorontravel). Mail me and I will be all ears for you.

Silences!

Sometimes silences become too heavy on the heart

We keep on sagging under the weight of those words

If they are believed or understood

Or even if they are unsaid…

Undressing Weakness

Battling mental health is like battling with your mind and
soul together

My anxiety is attention-seeking

My detailing needs love

My strengths have become a weakness

I feel marginalized in a large city

I feel alone in a vast group of people

I no more love ice-creams

I dislike to party anymore

I have buried my pain

Where no one is able to locate it

Feeling helpless

I hide in my house

Feeling neglected

Rejected, dejected...

I have stopped listening to music anymore

Every stitch of my body renders pain

Sadness, stress, disappointment, self-harm

My stomach churns, my hand shiver, acid burns

My heart seeks interaction

But mind can't withstand this circumference

Breaking the myths

I broke the mirror of anxiety

Depression is a liar

The devil puts a gun on your shoulder

Telling you all the wrong things to do

Hypnotizing your mind

It creates fear and anger

Gradually it makes you feel

All wrong is right

Self-harm is needed

But…

 You have the power to question

You have the power of positive energies

You have the power to beat the devil

And question the fear in you

Question the loss you anticipated

Fear is afraid of questioning

And mental health should be fearless

Once fearless, no anxiety, no depression

Just a happy soul…. Healthy soul… free bird.

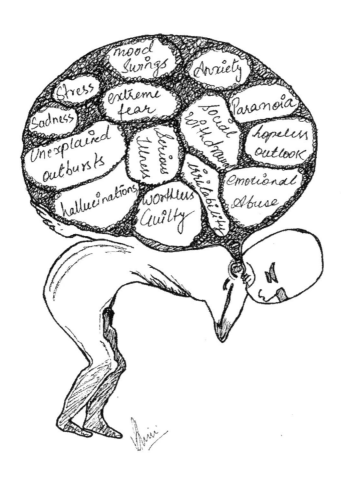

Enough For Life

You can only have enough

Which I let you have….

I'm Fugitive To My Thoughts

The wounded body of her, gives

me a sense of the killing;

She curated all her courage and gave all to me.

Somehow her bones were able to hold me.

Gently, I gave my hand to her.

The static hum of violent thunder

from her breath gave me jitter;

When it rained I gave her massage to

soothe her muscles.

Her body was all broken,

Her mind was shattered and devastated.

The flesh of her body was getting heavy day-by-day,

She tells me one day I can't come to life again,

As you will have to take me to my death slowly and softly.

He, in his thoughts, said how tough

it is to see your lover;

Besides you, withering from life's substance,

With her permission, I took her in my arms,

I then took my hand to her waist, making her feel secure;

I was careful about my touch, which was to make her feel,

Cared about not touching a healing body,

Her fear windows were open,

Her cramped corners were opening with tilt.

She jolts in herself and saw a sudden change;

With his hands caring for her

Her body was digging the pain

And letting her cry out loud.

Her fleeting hands were smooth and shaky

She never felt this good ever, which she was feeling in his

arms being cared for;

This transient in her was because of him.

He has seen her in the momentum of bursting out loud,

Screaming to the high, sobbing in the parking lots;

Sitting alone in the washroom for hours,

Swallowing her own feet and hands in a trance.

Now she is with me

She is in me

My fugitive arms are her life.

We both now fit in a twin-sized bed, entangled;

Survive together in the brutal world.

Let It Go…

Recovery is

Like climbing an abyss

Like making a new art

Like letting go

Like stop chasing your fear

The moment you accept you are in pain

Recovery is easy

The moment you realize that nothing is permanent

Recovery comes easy

You are less likely to get tapped by negative energies

You can fill your emptiness with a new version of you

****

Do Not Carry The Burden

Do not carry the burden of every hand

Do not carry the weight of every voice

That lets you down

That lets you feel worthless

What you are responsible, is to

Release it to the universe

I don't want you to understand my struggle

As you are not me, and vice-versa

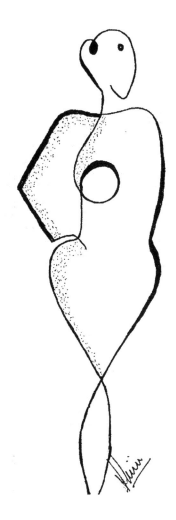

That, Someone Is In Me

I'm letting it go

As someone whom I love

Is getting hurt

And that

Someone

Is in me

****

All About Love Letters

What is the most enchanted,

love letter you have come across

Maybe the whole point of writing love letters?

Is not loving someone every time

Or maybe it is not to love many

Or get mushy-mushy

But at least revealing your devotion and your passion

To yourself, can be drafting a love letter

Another is to capitulate to the

other person's point of view

To dig deep into the soul

Releasing the fears, the torture,

the enjoyment, the voluptuous craving

The mysteries and endeavors.

Walking down the lane together is like writing a love letter to the known

I will wait for mine…

The Law Of Change

Once upon a time
I was the one who
Wanted to change the world around me,
Now, I admit,

That I'm changing myself,
As I gain wisdom;
I now know that
Changing the world
Will not help.
Rather be wise
And change the inner you.

****

Can You Un-Feel It? After You!

After you are bygone

Realizing all my gloom

After you are gone

Will not help

Or will it?

Or if I shelve it in my book

Will it make a difference?

Learning about my vulnerability

After you are gone

Will it settle the purpose?

If I write what you took from me

Will you be able to read it?

If I chat about my daydreams with you

After you are moved

Would they be attained after you?

The time drifted

The more it passes

The more it takes away from me

More importantly

If I feel it

Can you un-feel it?

Now I have left with merely you

After you…

lost and found!

Let's Dance Whole Night

Let's dance the wholesome night

Under the misty midnight

Let's enjoy the trance of moonlit

Let's get stoned under the moonshine

And…

Wake up naked under the shimmering sun

Next morning…

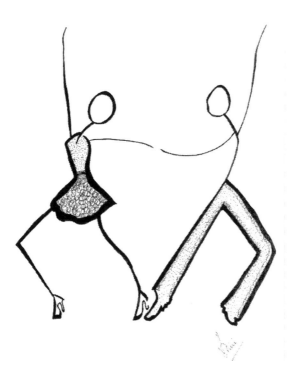

Moon Quizzed Sun

The chorus of sun and moon

Moon quizzed sun

How can I be remembered in your dreams?

I rise in dark

You remain in shine

Sun replied;

I die every night to let you breathe

They watch me

They fear my storm

But you are companion for lonely

You are the keeper of dark secrets

For my lady love!

******

Honey, Let's Radiate Together

She was inquisitive to realize

What?

She was curious to analyse

Thinking…

Will he dazzle with her?

Will he sparkle the success with her?

As he never acknowledged himself

An essential element for his own life

She pursued;

She convinced,

She used all her attempts,

By hook and crook;

And was ripped apart.

For he was still perturbed,

Not showing acceptance towards him deeds;

Was killing her

Because she was in him.

One day….

In his arms, snuggled and cuddled

She said;

Honey, let's radiate together

For the moon cannot radiate without sun

Likewise!

Growing Older

Let me tell you one thing

He whispered to her

Sitting cozy and warm

I'm getting old

I think I have overgrown

I'm ageing decently though, I think

She asked how did you know

That this happened to you

He replied;

The young girls are no more afraid

To open doors for me

The metro and rail ticket offers cheap pass

Women feel safe with me

They are no longer apprehensive of me

Alone in elevators

My farts are no longer recognized shady

Kids accept me more seriously

On the account of me being ageing

My yells are no longer taken as arrogant

And…

You have become more generous towards me

When I get drained while making love

She replied;

I thought your memories are fading honey

But with age you have become wiser

You are not growing old

You are growing old with me!

About the Author

#authorontravel #spiritedblogger #mavericksoul #lovevsweed #spoiledink #mysticart

She is on Google by all these and of course she is the author of the book and an eminent personality that strikes the balance in life. Being a single mother she has roamed several cities in India and abroad. She is a nomad and a solo traveler who inspires everyone with her blogs **(www.spiritedblogger.com).** Her story telling and poetic voice has captured many hearts in the past and has been featured with top-notch bookstores and publishers. She has been a part of various Lit Fests like NEx8, Delhi Book Fair, Jaipur Literature Fest, and others online. She especially enjoys the open mics and live sessions on Instagram. Her writing skills are used in the form ghost writing, ghost editing, blogging and content creation services.

The world is captivated for their love of poems and books. It is not only the people who are into this field but it is also the whole bunch of individuals who connects themselves with poems, quotes, phrases, verses and prose.

She is brilliant in her capabilities. Just with her debut book last year, she is rolled it again with another. You guys can wait for her trilogy of her books, well, this is a surprise wait for it to come.

****

Gratitude

Everything comes to you in the right moment. Be patient. Be grateful.
-Buddha

I would like to pay my gratitude to all of you who have been supporting me knowingly and unknowingly in my journey. Sometimes the simplest things mean the most. The readers who have appreciated my work and the ones who have been silent but loved the work I did, my humble gratitude to those. I appreciate all the encouragement given to me post my first book was launched and continuous support extended for this book as well. Encouragement is beyond material gifts and mentions. Thus, I'm thankful to the one who has been unconditionally supported me thought out the process, with my every highs and lows. **Gratitude is meaningless until it is shared. I'm thankful to the energies and the universe.**

References and Sources

Creator unknown All the images are hand drawn by the author. Creative representation. Retrieved from 01 October 2020.

Author Unknown. Mental health in India Date retrieved from website Dated 01 October 2020.
http://origin.searo.who.int/india/topics/mental_health/about_mentalhealth/en/

Author Unknown. Mental Health Information. Date retrieved from website Dated 01 October 2020. https://www.nimh.nih.gov/index.shtml

M. Angelou (1928–2014) Date retrieved from website Dated 01 October 2020. https://www.poetryfoundation.org/poets/maya-angelou

M. Angelou (1928–2014) Date retrieved from website Dated 01 October 2020. http://mayaangelou.com/

Men are from Mars Women from Venus. Book By Gray. J. Date retrieved from website Dated 01 October 2020.
https://www.amazon.in/dp/B006UN3K4O/ref=dp-kindle-redirect?_encoding=UTF8&btkr=1

B. B. Elizabeth Written by The Editors of Encyclopaedia Britannica. Date retrieved from website Dated 01 October 2020.

https://www.britannica.com/biography/Elizabeth-Barrett-Browning

TaNaK / Old Testament Epic Narrative, Narrative, Poetry, Prophetic, Prose Discourse, Wisdom. Date retrieved from website Dated 01 October 2020.

https://bibleproject.com/explore/tanak-old-testament/

Author Unknown. Forbidden Fruit. Fall of a Man. Adam and Eve. Grapple. Date retrieved from website Dated 01 October 2020.

https://en.wikipedia.org/wiki/Adam_and_Eve

Journals. Series: The Journals of Thomas Merton. Date retrieved from website Dated 01 October 2020.

https://www.librarything.com/series/The+Journals+of+Thomas+Merton

Read her previous work:

Beautiful compilation of short poems and prose. Available at Amazon and Flipkart worldwide. (EBook and paperback).

Words Unsaid…

Printed in Great Britain
by Amazon

14553934R00105